How to Buy a Used Motorcycle
Copyright © 2019 by Harley Callan

No part of this publication may be reproduced, distributed, or transmitted in any form or by any means, including photocopying, recording, or other electronic or mechanical methods, without the prior written permission of the author, except in the case of brief quotations embodied in critical reviews and certain other non-commercial uses permitted by copyright law.

Tellwell Talent
www.tellwell.ca

ISBN
978-1-77370-668-9 (Paperback)
978-1-77370-669-6 (eBook)

This book would not have been possible without the help of Bruce (Clarance) Bodiam and Melanie Gilbart. Many thanks.

CONTENTS

6	GLOSSARY
8	INTRODUCTION
11	THINGS TO CONSIDER WHEN BUYING YOUR MOTORCYCLE
12	SETTING A BUDGET
13	PLACES TO LOOK FOR USED MOTORCYCLES
14	SETTING UP THE APPOINTMENT
15	INSPECTING THE BIKE VISUALLY
16	CHECKING THE BIKE OVER STARTING WITH THE TIRES FIRST
18	CHECKING THE BRAKES (DISC AND DRUM)

22	CHECKING THE FORK SEALS
24	CHECKING STEERING HEAD BEARINGS
25	CHECKING SWING ARM BUSHING
26	CHECKING WHEEL BEARINGS
27	CHECKING THE SHOCKS
28	CHECKING THE ELECTRICAL
29	CHECKING THE HEAD & TAILLIGHTS, SIGNALS, HORN AND BRAKE LIGHTS
30	THE ROAD TEST
31	SIMPLE TOOLS NEEDED

GLOSSARY

ENGINE SIZE – measured in cubic inches (cc) i.e. 100,125,200 etc.

BRAKE PADS – steel backed plates with friction material bound to the surface

MASTER CYLINDER – control device converts no hydraulic pressure into hydraulic pressure

CALIPER DISC – squeezes pair of pads against disc rotor to show rotation of shaft

BRAKE SHOES – ridged curved plate with friction producing material tightened against the inside of a brake drum to produce a braking action

FRONT FORKS – connects motorcycle's front wheel and axle to its frame via triple champs

FORK SEAL – Keeps oil in lower legs for in use as hydraulic shock absorbing

STEERING HEAD BEARINGS – axis about which the steering mechanism (fork, handlebars, front wheel) pivots

SWING ARM – main component of rear suspension, used to hold rear axle firmly while pivoting vertically to allow suspension to absorb bumps in road

WHEEL BEARINGS – allows wheel to rotate supports motorcycle weight

SHOCKS – mechanical or hydraulic device designed to absorb damp shock impulses

CLUTCH – mechanical device that engages and disengages the power to transmission when motion must be controlled

INTRODUCTION

Let me start by introducing myself. My name is Harley Callan and I bought my first motorcycle when I was thirteen years old. I was drawn to motorcycles watching other riders on bikes with the freedom to just take off and go and explore places.

This was accomplished by working for my uncle on a farm for the entire summer in lieu of wages to purchase the bike. It was a step thru fifty Honda 1967 -a very collectable bike now. When the work day was over, I would ride it around on the farm without a care and boy, what a blast to simply be able to just go.

My uncle's suggestion was that the bike was a good size to start with, to learn how to ride safely and he was usually right. It was cheap on fuel, no repairs were needed and it always started. My father rode a Harley back in 1935 or 40 and I suppose that's where my desire came from. It was in my veins, so to speak. That, and being given the name Harley, a life immersed in motorcycles was meant for me.

As the following years passed, I bought and sold each bike when I felt I was ready for the challenge of a bigger one. Each used motorcycle I bought was in average or poor condition. I meticulously cared for each of them by cleaning, polishing, detailing, changing some parts to make them look and ride like new. Typically I would ride it for a season or so then sell it in the spring to get top dollar to invest in my next bike. In forty five years of riding, I acquired only three brand new bikes. The first was the classic Honda Mini Trail fifty, then at nineteen a 1974 Kawasaki Z1 900 -wow, what a bike, top speed was 145 mph.

Finally, in 2005 when my sons were home visiting, they said, when are you buying the new Harley you've longed for over the past 20 years? We just don't want a picture of you on one, go and get that bike you've always wanted. The very next day, my wife and I went and bought my 2005 Harley Ultra Classic.

At age 19 I chose to enroll as an apprentice mechanic at a bike shop. The requirement was to work alongside a licensed mechanic for approximately 4 years. During this time, I was educated on every single aspect of servicing all makes and models of motorcycles big and small, understanding functions of the engine, transmission, carburetors -every facet of motorcycles inside and out. New bikes have fewer problems whereas mechanical complications arise with older motorcycles.

Sometimes even a seemingly small issue can cause majorly poor running conditions or not allow it to start at all. Remembering the basics of how the engine works is key.

37 years and later and after I retired, I thought about writing this book and in doing so, would help other motorcyclists to be informed when buying a used bike. Before this book, I put together an 8 week course and taught at a college in the evenings. The course was designed to teach the basic mechanisms of how the motorcycle functions as well as some of the maintenance they could perform themselves with the proper tools and instructions. The response was overwhelming! Back then I longed to teach more but life had other plans for me. Now, I feel it is time to share my expertise with riders who are looking to purchase a used bike -to know what to look for and expect.

THINGS TO CONSIDER WHEN BUYING YOUR MOTORCYCLE

People are always asking how I go about buying a good used bike. Well, with graduated licensing now, the cost of insurance will be affected by the type of motorcycle you choose to purchase. This later reduces in cost when you acquire your full M license. To start with, a smaller size bike is easier to handle and learn on and is the least expensive to insure. Next, consider whether it will be used for pleasure or as a main form of transportation i.e. daily driving to and from work. This will also affect your insurance.

Statistics show there are greater chances of accidents to and from work. With that being said, your bike size should be between 200 cc and 400 cc. It could be a single cylinder or twin (2 cylinders) which will keep insurance premiums down to a minimum. If you have an M license, take a refresher course recognized by the insurance company and it will enable you to get a good discount. Insurance companies only insure for a year at a time not 6 months so premiums are a little higher. However, with a clean driving record, the right sized motorcycle and a successfully completed riding course, you should get the best rate going.

SETTING A BUDGET

First thing to consider is carefully setting a budget ahead of the purchase. Why? Because when you are done buying the bike without a budget set in place, selling the bike being unable to afford to ride is hugely disappointing...big time. Let's start with the cost of the bike then find out if it has been safetied. If not, the repairs can add up quickly or, if it needs a part in order to run properly, the cost of the part can be a surprise. Other costs to budget for include: sales tax at time of purchase, a license plate, a valid sticker and, of course, insurance.

Other items you will need or should have are proper boots, jacket, gloves and most importantly a good helmet.

PLACES TO LOOK FOR USED MOTORCYCLES

Today the internet is a big help compared to years past. You can view a lot of motorcycles at once and see the photograph also. In earlier years, you only had the newspaper and dealerships. With this in mind, you are best to create a list and narrow it down to the top five you are interested in otherwise it can lead to confusion and you end up buying the wrong bike.

Usually on the internet, you get a photo and a description typically stating the year, mileage, condition and cost. Be cautious though, sometimes people use what's called pasting where they take a copy of a perfect bike the use that as the photo. When you go to see the bike, it is nothing like what was depicted in the picture. It is a waste of time and money for you, not to mention frustrating. Therefore, the next bike you look at could be the real deal but potentially your frustration from the previous experience could lead to unintentional expression of doubt and irritating the current seller and potentially costing you the deal on a bike that was right for you. Auctions are another option or estate sales, again, keeping your entire budget in mind. If the bike is in running condition and you are able to test drive it, that would provide you with a lot of information.

SETTING UP THE APPOINTMENT

Most sellers prefer to schedule an appointment for the motorcycle viewing on the weekend where there is more time. This gives them a chance to discuss their pride and joy and explain the history of the bike. Making a cold call over the phone when you first contact the seller or sending an email especially if you make an offer that is below market value can be insulting to the seller. He may not respond at all in which case, you may be missing out on a really good deal or the seller may stay firm on his price and not give you a chance to negotiate the price. In past experience, it is best to go with setting up a time to view the bike and be able to check it over well to ensure you are satisfied with the bike in all aspects, then negotiate a price.

INSPECTING THE BIKE VISUALLY

First, when you meet the seller, introduce yourself to break the ice so to speak. With that done, you are visually going to look over the bike. At this time, look at the condition of the paint -is it damaged, scratched or faded, are all the painted parts in place? If a cover is damaged or missing you may not find another or have to pay a high price to get a replacement. Remember the budget, it all adds up to more costs. Ask to open the gas tank, take a small flashlight and look inside for any rust or rusting starting. This will lead to future fuel problems and bad running conditions. Again, more costs in the future.

Now, take a walk around the bike looking for any scrapes (I will call this road rash) where the bike has gone down on the road and has been scraped up. Typically, this can be seen on the ends or the sides of the mufflers or at the ends of the handlebars. If you see a newer part replaced inquire as to what happened. It could have just fallen over which is not a big deal but if it is damaged on the lower sides of the engine covers it could result in future problems.

CHECKING THE BIKE OVER STARTING WITH THE TIRES FIRST

Put the bike on the main center stand then look closely at the sideway of the tires. What you are looking for are cracks in the rubber indicating aged tires, these will not pass a safety let alone being safe to ride on.

Next, take a tire depth gauge and measure the depth of the tire in the middle if they measure less than 3/32 of an inch, the will not pass a safety. Following that, look for the date the tires were manufactured. This is found on the sidewall and if it is older than 4 years, it will be considered unsafe because the rubber becomes hardened. Ultimately, it will not have good contact with the road and may cause loss of control resulting in an accident.

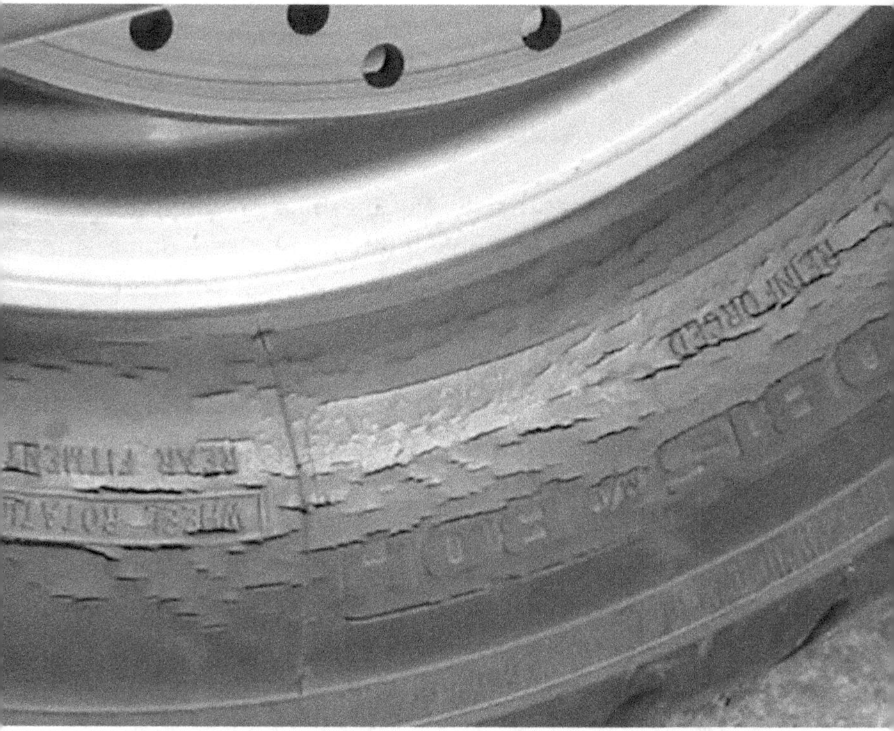

Cracked motorcycle tire

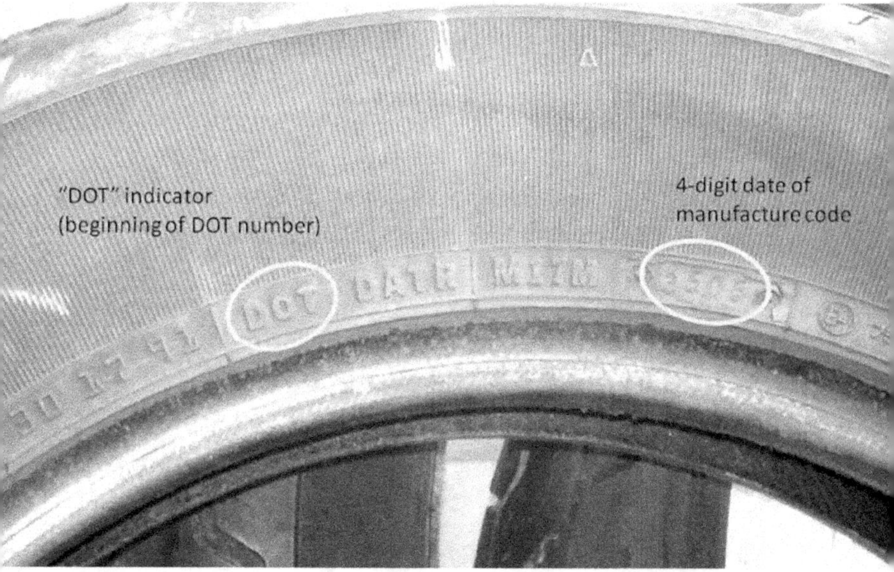

"DOT" indicator
(beginning of DOT number)

4-digit date of manufacture code

Date of tire manufacturer

CHECKING THE BRAKES
(DISC AND DRUM)

This can be done easily. Put the bike on the main center stand and first look at the front brakes. Some have two brake calipers others have one. What you are looking for is the brake pad thickness that is in the caliper. There is a line you will see on the pad if the pad is down to the line. (Minimum thickness 1.5mm) they will need to be replaced as it will not pass the safety standard. Next, look at the rubber brake lines that run from the master cylinder to the front brakes. What you are looking for are cracks or deteriorating defects in the rubber usually caused by age. If they are worn they need to be replaced and the brakes re-bled. This same inspection applies to the rear brakes. This is how to check disc brakes usually on bikes made after 1968 or '69. When checking brakes, also make sure the wheels spin freely after the brake has been released. If they don't, you may have a problem. This would indicated that the piston in the calipers have become semi-seized and are not releasing to fix it. In this case, the calipers have to be rebuilt. The seals are not pricey but require a lot of labour. If the pistons are corroded they will need to be replaced also.

You may find a motorcycle with drum or shoe type brakes. Some are still used on smaller model bikes but typically they are found on pre 1974 motorcycles. To check these types of brakes, you will find a pointing locator behind the brake arm and drum.

To check the brakes, apply them and watch how far the indicator moves in its travel range. If it travels the full range, chances are you will need new shoes. Another thing to note is that the dot on the brake arm and indicator are aligned. Sometimes the arm gets moved to get longer life out of the brakes which is incorrect and will give you a false indication that the brakes are still in good condition. In this case, it is important to make sure what you are looking for because and again, to be able to make this repair, the part and labour will add up in the total cost at the end and need to be included within your budget.

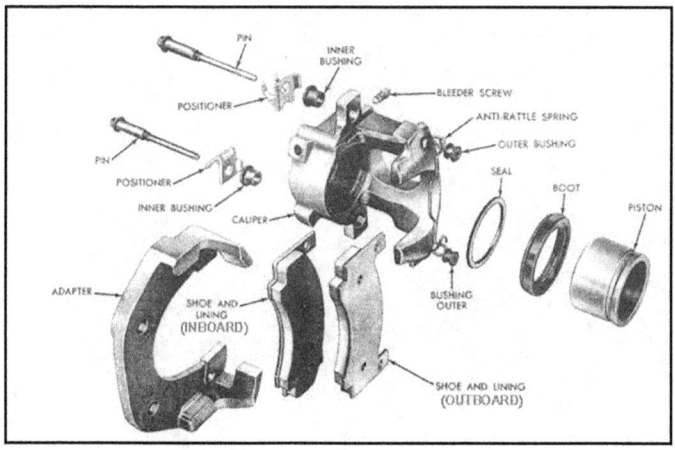

Disc brake

Drum brake

CHECKING THE FORK SEALS

This is an important required safety item on the bike because of leaks. If the seals are leaking badly enough the fork oil runs down onto your disc brakes causing you to lose breaking ability. First, look around the top part of the lower leg where they are for any leaking. Next, take a small screwdriver and pry up the dust seal that covers the seal.

If you see wetness then the seals are leaking and need to be replaced. Parts are inexpensive but labour, not so much as the fork have to come off of the bike and be taken apart entirely. At this time, look closely at the upper for tubes which are made of chrome for scratches or chips more so where they travel in and out of the lower for leg if they are scratched or chipped, they will also need to be replaced as will cause leaking even after new fork seals have been installed.

Leaking fork seals

CHECKING STEERING HEAD BEARINGS

First, put the motorcycle on the center stand. Following that, have someone at the rear of the bike holding it down to raise the front wheel off of the ground. This will allow you to move the handlebars back and forth to see if the bearings are notched in the steering head of the frame. Another way to check this is to point the wheel straight and allow them to turn to either side. If they stay in the straight, the bearing may be notched.

If this is found to be so, then they will need to be replaced which involves taking the front end off of the bike and changing the bearings in the neck of the frame. Bearings are approximately $100.00 and labour is a lot more again, keep in mind the budget –it all adds up. One more check, go to the front of the bike and grab each lower fork leg. Try to move them back and for the while watching for movement in the neck area. If there is, the bearings could be loose and, if you tighten them then they may show their true condition and be notched.

CHECKING SWING ARM BUSHING

Once again, put the motorcycle on the center stand then go to the back of the bike on the left hand side, kneel down, grab the wheel and the end, visualize approximately the 9 o'clock position and try and move the wheel side to side while looking at the swing arm area. If you feel movement or see movement, the swing arm bushings are worn and need replacing. This repair is costly for the reason of time involved to do the job plus parts. It is usually not found because the bushings are made of better materials on newer motorcycles.

CHECKING WHEEL BEARINGS

With the motorcycle on the main center stand, start with the rear wheel. Kneel down and grab the wheel at the 12 O'clock and 6 o'clock position and try to move the wheel back and forth. If movement is felt, chances are the wheel bearings need to be replaced. You can repeat the same test on the front wheel to check it's wheel bearings. Another means to check on bearings is to roll the wheel around and listen for any crunching noises. If this is heard, they may need replacing. On early models, pre 1990, the bearings could be knocked out and new ones installed. Post 1990 models were changed to being a press fit requiring the bearings to be pressed out of the wheel and allow for the new ones to be pressed back in. Therefore, it would cost more money for bearings and labour.

CHECKING THE SHOCKS

To start with, visually inspect the shocks for any leaks in the inner shock surrounded by the spring. Next, look at the bushing where they mount to the frame to see if the bushings are in good shape and appear tight. The next step is to sit on the bike and bounce up and down on the seat to see how the shocks rebound. If they rebound easily they may be losing their ability to dampen and may need replacing.

The shocks not only absorb the bumps you travel over but also control the stability of the bike as you are riding through curves in the roads and therefore effect the way the bike handles overall.

CHECKING THE ELECTRICAL

Start with locating the battery which usually is under the seat or behind a side cover. Take your meter, turn it to the dc scale (approximately 20 scale), put the red probe on the positive (+) side of the battery and the black probe on the negative (-) side of the battery then read the volts. It should read 12 to 12.5 volts. This tells you the battery is fully charged and appears to be good.

Now let's check the charging system. Start the bike up, let it warm up if not already warm and put your meter back on the same way as indicated above, then, raise the engine speed up to approximately 2000 rpm. At this point the meter should read 14.2 volts which would indicate the charging system is working well. A charging system maintains a constant 12 volts to the battery to support the electrical running of the bike for example, the lights, and ignition and so on. If you do not get that reading you may have a charging problem which can lead to expensive repairs.

Therefore you are wise to check this when purchasing a motorcycle of any size as parts are costly and can be difficult to get a proper diagnosis.

CHECKING THE HEAD & TAILLIGHTS, SIGNALS, HORN AND BRAKE LIGHTS

First, turn on the key and check to see that the headlight and taillight are on. You will see it lit up on the left side of the handlebar, a switch marked H and L meaning high/low beam. Move it up and down to see if each beam is functioning. When you switch to high beam a blue light will come on in the instrument cluster between your speedometer and tachometer telling you the high is on but check to see if is on at the light also. Then switch it to the low beam and check to see if is on in the headlight. Next, look to see the taillight is also on. Now, push the button marked horn to see it is working –get ready for a startling noise.

Following that, try the signals (it will be marked 'signals') push the switch to the L for left and check that the front signal and rear are flashing. It will also show up again in your instrument cluster showing which one you have chosen. Next, move the switch to the R for right and check those signals front and back. Now you want to check your front and rear brake light switches. With the key on, squeeze the front brake lever and check to see if the taillight has become brighter. This tells you the front switch is working. To check the rear switch, depress the rear brake pedal and look to see that the taillight has again become brighter indicating that that switch is working well. If either switch is not working it will have to be repaired in order to pass a safety check.

THE ROAD TEST

This is where it becomes tricky as you are assuming responsibility for the bike if you take it out for a test ride. In other words, if you drop the bike or damage it in any way, essentially you have bought it. A lot owners are not willing to let you road test the bike for this exact reason and typically, an add will state 'no test pilots'. Unfortunately, you can only see how the bike runs by driving it. With that said, if you are able to take it out for a test ride, do so to see how the bike runs to ensure that it is smooth and quiet and shifts well through the gears.

When you get back, stop, put the bike in either 2nd or 3rd gear and slowly let out the clutch with a minimum amount of throttle. The bike should almost stall out indicating the clutch is in good shape. If this is not the case, you may have a clutch slippage problem that may need adjusting. Park the bike on the side or center stand and walk around doing a visual check of the bike looking for any oil leaks or gas leaks and that the motor is relatively quiet and running smooth which they should be.

The next step is the price negotiation. If there are a few minor repairs needed, and you are aware of the costs of said repairs, this could work in your favour in getting a better price. Always get a bill of sale stating price, deposit and balance owing.

SIMPLE TOOLS NEEDED

MULTIMETER: The multimeter measures voltage and state of charge across the battery and is available at most automotive stores.

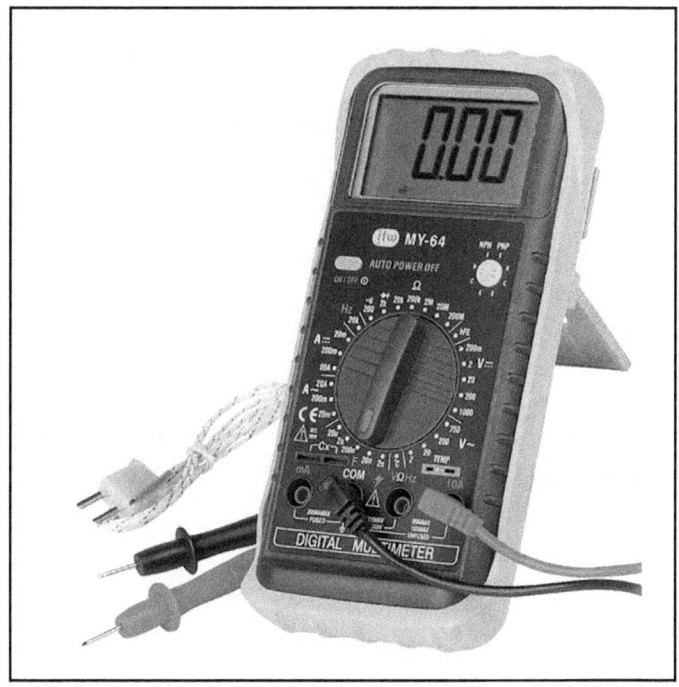

Digital multimeter

TIRE DEPTH GAUGE: The tire depth gauge measures the depth of the rubber and is available at most automotive stores.

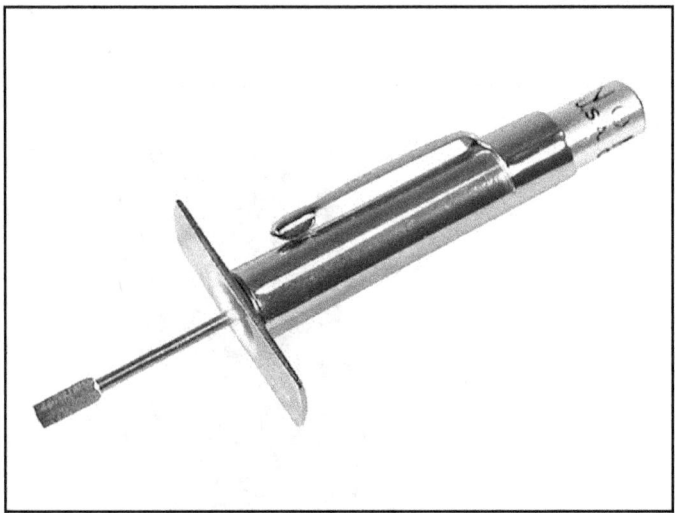

Tire depth gauge

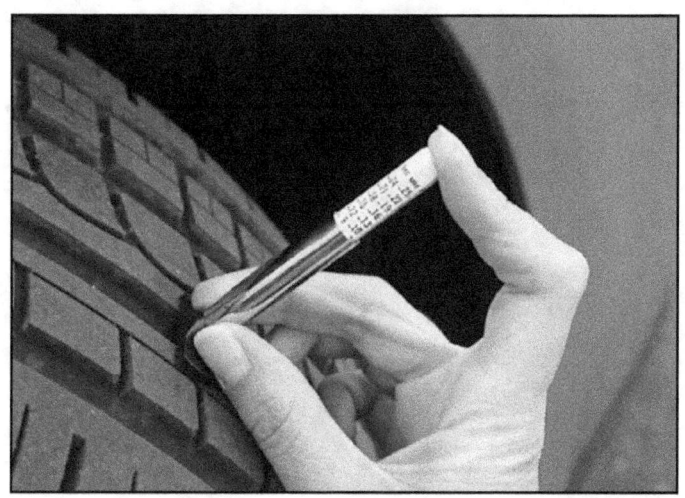

Tire depth gauge application

www.ingramcontent.com/pod-product-compliance
Lightning Source LLC
LaVergne TN
LVHW011901060526
838200LV00054B/4461